A Zondervan/Ladybird Bible

Jesus the Friend

By Jenny Robertson
Illustrated by Alan Parry

ZONDERVAN
PUBLISHING HOUSE

OF THE ZONDERVAN CORPORATION
GRAND RAPIDS, MICHIGAN 49506

"Mary, what shall we do? We've run out of wine!" It was a terrible disgrace to run out of wine at a wedding, but Mary told Jesus about it. Then she spoke to the servants, "My son Jesus will help. Just do whatever He says."

Jesus told them to fill six huge jars with water. "Now take some out and give it to the best man," He said.

A servant filled the jug. He waited anxiously while the best man drank. Would he be angry at being offered water? But the best man smiled. "This is the finest wine I have ever tasted—imagine saving it till last!" Jesus had turned the water into wine so everyone could enjoy the party.

Large crowds followed Jesus wherever He went, and He taught them about God. He always spoke simply. He didn't make things difficult, the way some of their leaders did. Jesus told amusing, interesting stories explaining to the crowd that God loved them very much and they should always try to put God first in everything.

Jesus made the people very happy, but the priests were angry at His teaching.

One evening Jesus and His close friends decided to sail across Lake Galilee to find a quiet place away from the crowds. Jesus was tired, and He soon fell fast asleep. Suddenly a fierce wind blew up, and huge waves crashed over the sides of the little boat. Jesus' friends were terrified and hurried to wake Him up.

But Jesus was not afraid. "Be still!" He said to the storm. At once everything grew calm.

His friends were amazed. "Who can this man be?" they said to one another.

After this Jesus often made the leaders angry. One day four men brought a lame friend to the house where Jesus was, but they could not get in for the crowds. Determined that Jesus should help their friend, they made a big hole in the mud roof and lowered him through it.

Jesus looked at the man. "Everything you've done wrong is forgiven. Get up now and walk," He said. The man got up happily, and hurried out, praising God.

But the leaders were angry. "Only God can forgive people that way," they said.

It was a Saturday, the holy Sabbath, when people could not do any work. Jesus and His friends were walking through the fields.

Jesus' friends felt hungry, so they picked some wheat. The nutty kernels were delicious.

But some of the Jewish leaders saw them, and came over to Jesus. "Your friends are breaking the law! No one is allowed to work on the Sabbath! Picking wheat like that is working."

Jesus was angry. He knew that God made the Sabbath to be a time of rest when people could worship Him. But the leaders had made up so many rules that keeping the Sabbath day was a burden, not something to be enjoyed. Jesus explained this to them, but they were angry and would not listen.

"Jesus breaks our laws," they muttered.

One Sabbath, Jesus went into the synagogue to pray. There He saw a man with a paralyzed hand. Jesus knew that if He helped the man, the watching leaders would accuse Him of breaking the Sabbath law. But Jesus said, "If your sheep falls into a hole, you lift it out at once, even on the Sabbath."

Then Jesus told the man, ''Stretch out your hand.'' The man obeyed. At once his hand was well and strong. Jesus' enemies began making plans together to have Jesus put to death.

All day Jesus taught the people about God. When evening came, His friends asked Him to send the crowd away to find food. But Jesus said, "Give them food yourselves."

Andrew pushed a boy forward. "This child has five loaves and two fish," he said, "but that won't go very far!"

Quietly Jesus took the basket the boy offered Him. "Make the people sit down," He said to His friends. Then He thanked God for the food, and His friends passed it out among the people. Everyone had more than enough, even though there were over five thousand people! They were all amazed at Jesus' power.

Two sisters invited Jesus to their house. Martha went to do the cooking, but Mary sat down and listened to Jesus. Poor Martha was upset. "Make my sister come and help with the work," she said to Jesus.

But He replied, "Martha, you can cook dinners every day, but Mary is learning about God, and that is best."

Once Jesus and His friends came to a village and saw ten men standing by themselves at a safe distance from everyone else. The men were ill, and anyone who came too close might catch their illness, too. They begged Jesus to make them well.

Jesus told them to go and show a priest that they were better—this was what the law said they had to do. As soon as they started off, they became well again.

One man came back to say "Thank You" to Jesus. He told Jesus how pleased he was to be well again. Now he could go back to his family. He no longer needed to hide away from everyone.

"There were ten of you, and you're the only one who has come back to say 'Thank you,' " said Jesus. "Go on home," He told the happy man. "Your faith has made you completely well again."

"Let's take our children to see Jesus," some families said. They set off, but Jesus' friends tried to stop them. "Jesus is too busy to see children!" they said.

Jesus heard them and called, "Don't send them away. Let the children come to Me." He turned to the grown-ups. "You need to have faith like these children!" He told them, touching the children who crowded closely around Him. They ran home very happy because they knew how much Jesus loved them.

Tramp! Tramp! Tramp! A huge crowd walked past the blind beggar Bartimaeus, who sat in the dust at the roadside. "What's happening?" he called out.

"Jesus is coming!" cried the crowd. At once blind Bartimaeus began to shout, "Help me, Jesus! Help me!" Unkind people told him to be quiet, but he kept on shouting.

Then someone said, "Get up! Jesus heard your shouts. He wants you to come to him." Bartimaeus jumped up, and tottered forward to Jesus, his knobby fingers stretched out in front of him to guide him along. "What do you want Me to do for you?" asked Jesus, gently.

"Oh Teacher, I want to see!" said Bartimaeus breathlessly. He was overjoyed to hear Jesus say, "Your faith has made you see."

The blind man blinked. He looked up and saw the face of Jesus. Joyfully he followed Jesus along the road, singing and laughing as he thanked God.

The two sisters, Martha and Mary, had a brother named Lazarus. One day Lazarus became ill and within two days he died. Jesus was far away, but the two sisters sent someone to tell Him the news. When Jesus arrived at their house, Martha met Him and said, "If You had been here my brother would not have died. But I know that it's not too late to help him, even now. I know God will do whatever You ask him."

"Whoever believes in Me will live, even if he dies," Jesus said. "Do you believe this, Martha?"

"Yes," she answered him firmly. "Yes."

The body was in a cave, which had been closed up with a stone. Jesus told them to remove the stone. Then He prayed to God and called out loudly, "Come out, Lazarus!" Lazarus appeared at the entrance of the cave, alive but still wrapped in linen cloths.

"Unwind these cloths and let him go," said Jesus. Many people believed in Jesus now, but the priests decided the time had come to arrest Him. They watched Him carefully, waiting for their chance to seize Him.

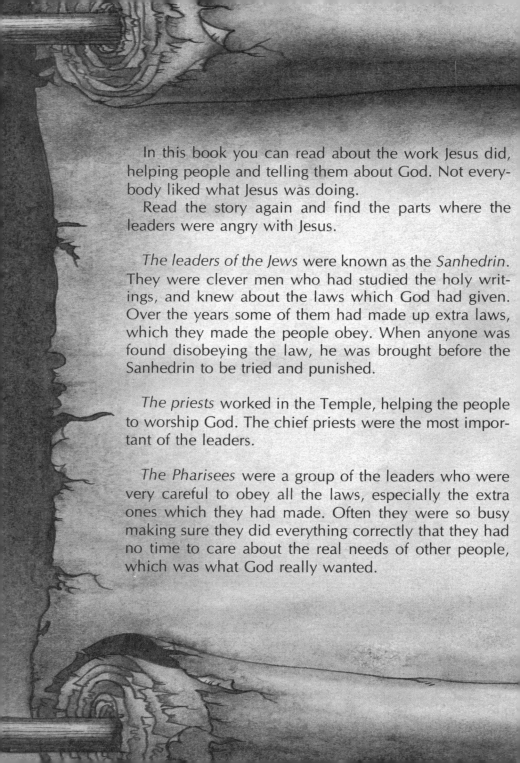

In this book you can read about the work Jesus did, helping people and telling them about God. Not everybody liked what Jesus was doing.

Read the story again and find the parts where the leaders were angry with Jesus.

The leaders of the Jews were known as the *Sanhedrin*. They were clever men who had studied the holy writings, and knew about the laws which God had given. Over the years some of them had made up extra laws, which they made the people obey. When anyone was found disobeying the law, he was brought before the Sanhedrin to be tried and punished.

The priests worked in the Temple, helping the people to worship God. The chief priests were the most important of the leaders.

The Pharisees were a group of the leaders who were very careful to obey all the laws, especially the extra ones which they had made. Often they were so busy making sure they did everything correctly that they had no time to care about the real needs of other people, which was what God really wanted.